FISHING THE CALM

FISHING THE CALM

POEMS BY

LUCINDA PARIS

Selected and edited by Anne Paris

Lucinda McMichael Paris

1937 – 2016

Sail on, silver girl

ACKNOWLEDGMENTS

The poems previously published were in a variety of small journals and compilations, and many of them are no longer in print. I did my best to track down copyrights and get permission to republish where needed. I am grateful to those who answered my inquiries about decades-old publications.

"After Reading *The Professor's House*" was previously published in *Poetry East*.

"Slow Dancing with a Burglar" was previously published in *Carolina Quarterly*.

"For a Hard Winter" was previously published in the *Crescent Review*.

"Night Tracings" and "Owl" were previously published in *Plainsong*. "Owl" also appeared in two books, *The Valley Beneath Words: The Best of Plainsong* and *Quiet Music: A Plainsong Reader*.

"Timuk's Wife, Spring" was previously published in *Plains Poetry Journal*.

"Hiking the Laurel River" was previously published in *Piedmont Literary Review*.

"Driving Highway 15-501" was previously published in *Hyperion* and is republished with permission.

"Fireflies" and "The Rimland" were previously published in *A Living Culture in Durham* and are republished with permission. "The Rimland" was also published in *Weymouth: An Anthology of Poetry*.

"Goldilocks" was previously published in *2006 Kakalak: An Anthology of Carolina Poets*.

"In a Peruvian Hammock" and "Fishing the Calm" were published in *Blue Pitcher* and are republished with permission.

Cover and author photo by John Staddon.

ISBN: 9798517550804

CONTENTS

EDITOR'S NOTE

My mother wrote a great deal of poetry, most of it in the 1970s and 1980s. Some of it was published, some of it was not, but all of it was very good. Lucinda Paris turned to short stories and a novel in the following decades, leaving poetry behind. This compilation is a way to honor her work for the fifth anniversary of her death.

I tried to be true to my mother's original intentions in putting together this book, but I'm sure I made choices she would not have made (starting with, but not limited to, creating this book). Any errors or missteps are mine.

Anne Paris

June 2021

AUTOBIOGRAPHICAL POEMS

We expect the first frost
at any time

BEFORE SUNRISE AT ATLANTIC BEACH

It is still dark.
We have left your father and mother
fitfully asleep.
Our son and daughter dreaming,
soon to be gone.
You and I are barefoot,
bundled against the chill,
walking to get a newspaper and coffee.
Too early. We feel the darkness,
the cold waves pulling something from us.
In the distance
the pier seems strung with lanterns.
The moon thins
and the stars are turning away.

Caught in the same sadness
we do not comfort each other.
Ahead tiny shorebirds
skate back and forth
on patches of wet sand,
receding from us
like lost chances,
children we'll never have.

We are close enough now to the pier
to see people fishing,
men and women standing alone,
families bunched together on benches.
Offshore, shrimp boats drift
on the deep water,
small beacons glowing
like cigarettes lit for comfort.
These are the lonely occupations.
Whoever you are,
come back to us.

BUILDING THE CHINESE RAILROAD

Fifteen years from
when I last heard him speak,
I recognize his voice –
my Chinese analyst.
Where I hear him speak
is beautiful in irony.
His unpronounceable l's
sound over the heads of the other parents
at the Boy Scout court of honor.
He has returned from Taiwan,
has married, has two sons.
I have returned from a marriage,
have married again, have a daughter
and a son.

When I saw him last
I gave him, finally, the present of a dream.
I thought that I would never see him again.

> Mainland China and miles of red clay,
> he and I in a crew working to build
> the Chinese railroad.
> Darkness closes in. We gather
> pine boughs. We lie down together.

He and I cry together in his office.
I leave.
He flies to Formosa.

His two sons and mine
hold candles in a darkened room,
speak the vows that old men in uniform
write for young boys to recite,
of honor among friends.
He and I are bound in such a way.
Across three rows of parents
we salute each other.

AT THE FLORENCE CRITTENTON HOME, NORFOLK

August 1963

The light and shadow
next to the river
are studies in pointillism,
Seurat's picnic without the men.
All the young women
are pregnant.
They dress in pastels
and move languidly
like balloons blowing
softly across the lawn.

Sarah, my friend,
comes toward me
in slow motion.
She is smiling and holds
a pleated paper fan
decorated with religious pictures.
She is the same Sarah
(we admire the fan
but not the pictures).
Her hair is damp
and lies upon her neck
in childish tendrils.

All the windows in the house
are open.
Someone is playing
Frere Jacques
on the parlor piano.

NIGHT TRACINGS

for Neal

You have called us out
this moonless summer night
to see the sycamore trees
in the lot beside our house
blazing white with fireflies.

You have called us
from the ordinary.
I dry my hands on my apron.
Charlie was shaving.
He is barechested,
a towel around his neck.
Anne, in her nightgown,
still holds the book
she was reading.

We have never seen
the sycamores lighted
quite like this,
the fireflies signalling
in such legions,
the females calling,
the males following
their glittering
bioluminescent lead.

We stand here
moist from the heat,
star struck, quiet,
caught together
for one of the last times.

As we walk back
toward the house,
to our diverging lives,
there is such comfort
having your arm
around my shoulder,
the path dark,
behind us the night
filled with these lights
that go on and on.

THE RIMLAND

Weymouth, May 1985

In the resinous forest
a thin snake,
a strip of braided beauty,
threads its way,
black on brown,
through the pine needles.
Where the path breaks
blackberry bushes,
muscadine vines
grow tangled.
This pasture is rinsed
in sunlight.
Every blade stands
separate.
A woodpecker
sets off a thrumming
steady and insistent
as the heart.
How thin, I think,
the membrane between
despair and joy.

TO CHARLIE IN MISSOULA

It is the time of year
when windshields deliver
the coup de grace
to tired butterflies.
Black wings banded in blue,
the monarch's gold wings
decorate the road home.
Persimmon trees are hung
with cotton candy webs
of caterpillars, and with fruit.

In the trees behind the house
this year's squirrels
practice independence,
fumbling branch to branch.
They stop.
Another noise in the forest.
They begin again.
Last night a small animal screamed
down in the creek bed,
giving the six-foot black snake
its last voice before winter.
The fall has not changed for us at home
but there is a sense of easing,
of letting down into life's proper order.

I see that what started out
describing autumn is instead
about your leaving.
We watch your weather report
each night on the late news
and wait for your letters.
The days here are like summer.
The nights drop thirty degrees.
We expect the first frost
at any time.

LAKE MATTAMUSKEET

In the twilight
we steered the bateau
around the edge of the lake
toward the lodge.
All day we had slapped insects,
joking that Mattamuskeet
was Indian for many mosquitoes.
We had counted a hundred turtles,
sixteen water snakes,
one eagle, one osprey, one owl,
painted buntings, indigos,
fish crows, kingfishers, hawks.
Our shoulders ached from poling
through the shallow water,
all our senses finally on hold.

The last light fell
behind the curtains of Spanish moss.
There was no noise
except the sound of our boat
bobbing in the still water.
A rush,
and the night was filled with egrets,
snowy egrets descending,
their wings folding,
unfolding, white upon white,
filling the black
scalloped branches of the cypresses,
a hundred candles
caught in some holy breath,
in our own breath,
resting, then suddenly rising
one at a time,
extinguishing themselves,
leaving that place
detached from the rest
of our lives.

RESEARCH POEMS

These building blocks
are clouds, mist, vapor

AFTER READING THE PROFESSOR'S HOUSE

One of the rewards, surely,
of growing older
is understanding that
nothing is simple,
finite, or, after all,
truly understandable.
Attempts to decode,
to marginate the universe,
prove useless.
Perhaps failing eyesight
is itself a tool.
Faces swim toward
each other
in a winter's afternoon.

In middle age
you thought the crow black.
Now he is shot with
iridescences.
What you thought crows
are cowbirds, starlings,
purple grackles. All share
a thousand ambiguities.
In flight, even the crow's wing,
seen from underneath,
is gray.

It is a comfort
not having to know everything,
not having to always assign
a correct name, the right color
to life's objects.
The process says, Trust me.
These building blocks
are clouds, mist, vapor,
sunsets assigned in blues
and lavenders – also magentas,
and washed in water.
Stars have no outlines.
Trust me.

SINGING ALEQUAAJIK'S SONG

1

Berry picking
On the high hillside
South wind at my back
Flowers the color of milk
Mixed with sunlight.

2

Down below in camp
The children play
The women chatter.
Out on the ocean
Men in kayaks
Bob like toys.

3

Laughter, singing
Travel up the hill to me.
The day is round
Sweet to the taste.

4

Yellow sunlight
Blue ocean
Soft green grass.
My tears rise
From a spring
I do not know.
My name is called
From no direction.
A great grief has come over me.

MONTEZUMA'S AVIARY

Before dawn the moon,
a piece of smooth white jade,
has set behind Tenochtitlan.
Montezuma crosses the terraces,
the stone courtyards,
unlocks the door to the aviary
with his gold key. The birds know him.
They stir and settle back into the darkness.
The quetzal bird opens one eye,
permits the hand gliding over its long tail,
that cascade of imperial feathers.
Montezuma murmurs to the hummingbirds,
hundreds of pairs who will flash by day,
gems pried from their silver settings.
The parrots are awake, their tongues silent
in their brilliant beaks.

Montezuma takes a small flagon of chocolate
from the pocket of his robe.
Standing beside the hanging cages of canaries
he watches through the aviary's bamboo bars
the morning light rising across the marshes.
He slowly drinks the chocolate.
Soon he will relock the door
and return to the palace to his bed.

Within the hour the aviary will become
a raucous world of reedy calls.
Three hundred men will clean the rookeries,
fill the water bowls, scatter seeds.
Women will harvest the feathers
falling from the moulting birds
to weave them into shields, standards
for battle. Now everyone still sleeps.

Montezuma rises each morning,
puts on his splendid cape of tiny feathers,
his headdress of royal green quetzal feathers,
his ornaments of hammered gold,
takes up his standard of a thousand feathers
and is the Sun.

MAUD GONNE

For the third time in my life
an English professor loses himself
to the vision of Maud Gonne
entering John Yeats' studio –
the apple blossoms
and all that heroic beauty,
six feet of it,
Willie's eyes upon her entrance,
center stage.
And for the third time
I am troubled by a Maud Gonne,
fierce for a free Ireland,
filling an entire train carriage
with her retinue of caged birds,
even, they say, a full-grown hawk
in precious plumage.

I suppose as a woman I find
so much beauty troubling
and would want it for myself.
But, more than that,
I can feel the cool among the feathers.
I picture her at another time
wearing a large-brimmed hat
dripping with pale egrets,
birds of paradise,
tiny finches.

TIMUK'S WIFE, WINTER

1

The day has been sleet
falling on black water
and nothing but the sound of sleet,
the dog's muted barking,
the runners of the sled
cutting through the heart like stone.

2

Outside these ice walls
the kayak lies in the snow.
The dogs sleep,
their backs toward the sea.

3

The last oil in the lamp burns,
making shadows on the rugs,
on the long line of your body.
Your dark eyes turn to me.

4

Timuk, brown bear,
hold me.
Brown owl, wrap your giant wings
around me.
Fish, put on your silver tail
and dance with me.

TIMUK'S WIFE, SPRING

1

It is the thaw.
Pieces of ice float downstream.
Ptarmigan scatter across the brown grass
like ivory beads shot from a necklace.
Now we go south
to the sea.

2

In the summer camp
yellow poppies grow to the water's edge.
The faces of the women
are laughing stones.

3

When you form the tent frame
do not trouble to make it larger.
You will not need the extra skins
scraped by my knife
shaped like the last half-moon.
This morning
my hand dipping down
caught blood again.

4

Small animals will brush past us
in the What-Is-To-Be.
Everywhere the sun
spins its long light.

DREAMS

What is stolen,
imagined,
given away

SLOW DANCING WITH A BURGLAR

Never mind that in the rooms
outside this room
they – whoever they are –
is it my mother or the Mafia
or part of myself –
are stuffing the silver,
the Venetian glass,
cloisonne,
my grandmother's emeralds,
even the chandelier,
into a sack.
The prisms ring and rustle
in alarm.

They have left a burglar
in my room to guard me.
He is a fat man who smokes cigars
(not my father who was thin
and smoked Russian cigarettes).
The room is growing darker
and, outside the window, lights
crop up across the city
like white flowers.
The man perspires.
He smells warm and damp.
Somewhere in the room
a radio plays
    Lady, morning's just a moment away
    And I'm without you once again
and then there is a moment that catches –
and we dance, he and I,
past the window, the lighted city,
away from what is stolen,
imagined,
given away.

RIDING IN THIS BOAT OF DREAMS

for Ann

Seining for stars
darting through the black water,
their quick tails
shining memories,
we are in a flotilla of boats,
little lanterns, each
with its nets cast wide and
falling in night's warm waters,
each cradled in the swells,
lulled and drifting.
Schools of stars
swim through the nets.
On either side
great manta wings lift, glide,
billowing like bedcovers,
eiderdown.
Porpoises, their arches silver
rising, returning,
usher the boats
through the shoreless sea,
their child-like voices calling,
Come. Come.
This is the comfort that should have been.

ESCAPING FROM PURDAH

Flying with a great sheet,
silken, billowing –
a sail held before them,
the women navigate
high over the rooftop gardens,
the locked gates,
the parapets of Sousa,
above the fertile valleys,
the mountains,
the melting snow.
Turning in unison,
not one of them asks
how they came to be in the same dream
or which of them is dreaming it.

Perfumed with jasmine
they have waited for years
behind tissued silks. No more.
All this past night
tiny bells have whispered,
summoning through empty chambers.
Eunuchs have spent the long night searching.
The one servant who might have told
has long since had her tongue cut out.
Even if she pointed to the sky
no one would look up to see the women
circling one last time over the palace walls.

Roosters sound an alarm.
Below, each woman sees her children
drowning kittens in the courtyard well.
She sees her father and brothers
for the first time in many years.
They are saddling their horses
to ride away.

HOTEL DREAM

It is an old hotel,
the wallpaper peeling,
pipes whistling through their rust.
In one corner of the room
a man in a red velvet robe is shaving.
Wizened little czarinas
huddle around a table
demanding tea from an enormous samovar
whose steam curls up and lies upon
the ceiling upside down.
Everyone talks of Old Russia –
sabers … cossacks … sables.
I fill the tall glasses with hot tea.

The old lady czarinas clap twice,
such power from their tiny hands,
and a gypsy tearoom orchestra
bursts through the door,
guitars and balalaikas strumming.
Red-sashed waiters bring food –
huge bowls of caviar, boiled eggs,
black bread, apple puddings,
wine jellies that wobble on the plate.
Someone pulls a vodka bottle
from a sleeve. Everyone drinks up.

The red Russian catches me
around my waist, pulls me into a dance.
The arthritic czarinas are thwacking
their canes on the tabletop
in time to the music,
making obscene gestures to the dancing man
who runs his hand down the front of my blouse.

The old women are frenzied now,
calling for more and more,
their boots stamping under the table,
their feeble fingers
unfastening their brooches,
throwing them at our feet.
Steam billows from the samovar.
The gypsies play faster, faster, faster.
How will this dream end?
Behind the curtains, beyond the window,
the moon reflects on miles of railway tracks
slipping away through the snowy night.

FISHING THE CALM

for Mary Clarke

Here
The silver surface of the water
Like glass
The silver hand line
Shining like an umbilicus
Through the surface of the sea
Quiet
The peaceful fisherman I
And slippery as a birth
You the child-sized
Grey-green seahorse
Parting the silver surface
The shining cord
You the mother
You the pouched father
I the peaceful fisherwoman
I the fishing man
You the silver-green seahorse
The shining sea.

DEIRDRE DREAMING

Early morning under the far fields
Mrs. Tiggy-winkle sets the table
with tiny cups and saucers,
tiny plates of bread and butter
on the white tablecloth.
The kettle is boiling on the fire.
Only the hour is unexpected.

You are Lucie come to tea
or your daughter Heather
come through the door behind the hill.
Mrs. Tiggy-winkle wipes her hands
on her clean starched apron.
She hugs you close.
She smells like peppermint.

You ask her to tell you what happens
to the secret places, the magic places
in a little girl's heart.
She begins to pour, and the tea
runs over the rims of the tiny cups,
onto the white cloth. She frowns
and will not answer.

She sees you now as you are.
You have asked one question
a child would never ask. "You must leave,"
she cries, "must leave, must leave!"
You are no longer Lucie come to tea
or your daughter Heather.
You are Deirdre dreaming.

THE YOUNGER LOVER

I am wearing my mother's tennis dress
but I am my age now.
We are on the lawn of a large estate.
You are stretched out, relaxed,
your head in my lap.
It is a summer evening.
The garden is full-blown,
blossoms hanging heavy over the pool;
carp hanging under the surface,
heavy as blossoms.
You wear white flannel pants,
a white linen shirt, three buttons
unfastened at the neck.
I am tracing the line of your chin,
the opening of your shirt
with my fingers.
There is such peacefulness with you.
It is like loving a child.
It is like being a child too.
It is like the peacefulness after making love
though I doubt if we ever shall.
The sun falls low behind the poplars,
drawing in all the colors of the garden.
I did not ask for this,
cannot be the one to ask for this to end.
Time slows.
You reach up to catch my hands
and hold them still.
At the far edge of the garden
the moon begins its gradual ascent.

FAIRY TALES

Flightless woman,
you must make a ladder of bones

GOLDILOCKS

The hidden path
Under the trees
Ferns and leaf mold
Dripping mist.
This is black
Deep childhood.

The house on the forest floor
Dark green shutters
Wooden shingles.
Inside
Red wooden chairs
The table set for three
And on a blue cloth
Thick white bowls
Porridge
And a pitcher of cream,

Three beds upstairs
Feather mattresses
Soft rain blowing through
The curtains. Sleep.

And then
The bears are in the room
Quarreling.
The baby sulks in the corner
The mother weeps.
She buries her face
In her apron.

You rise to leave.
The father bear approaches you
He turns your body in his arms
He holds your back to his body
He leans over you
And whispers
I have missed you
I need you
Stay.

THE ENCHANTED PIG

You have travelled through great sadness,
wearing out pair after pair of iron sandals
crossing the boundaries of your father's kingdom.
Here in the thick forest, a tower without windows,
its door on the roof. Flightless woman,
you must make a ladder of bones to reach it,
must wait in its empty room, remembering.

You had no choice. Your father's secret book
held the sentence, "The youngest daughter
of this king will marry a pig from the north."
Your sisters married princes
while you waited for this strange fate,
this pig to come a-wooing. He did.

After he had spoken for you
in his resonant, porcine voice,
after the royal wedding and the wine,
you drove away together in his carriage
to a tiny gatehouse at the edge of a bog.
Before entering the house,
the groom rolled in the black mud,
giving low grunts, low moans.
You took out your handkerchief
and wiped his snout. You kissed him.
He sighed.

All that night high winds
wound through the trees.
Heavy drops of rain pelted
the house in the forest.
You turned to him for comfort
and found more.
"Oh truffle me, truffle me, do,"
you cried. He did.

Your sisters wrote complaining.
Their princes slept like soldiers,
snoring, oblivious to them.
Each night was everything to you.
But these stories have a turn.
Happiness is never enough.
Some wicked woman comes to tell you
the truth. Here is the string
to bind his hoofs, to lift the curse.
Your husband slept and woke to find
you circling him with string. He left.

Now you find yourself in this high room
without windows, staring at that one door.
Passion has come from far off,
farther than you have come, to find you,
to bend you at the knees, at your waist,
to make you servile and alone.
What is the point in asking for what you want?
Ah, but listen. Listen.
Has he returned in another form?
Great wings flutter at the little door.

THE TWELVE DANCING PRINCESSES

What now, Star Gazer?
Now that you have seen her sisters
straight-backed in their little boats,
the twelve enchanted young men
rowing them across the moonless water,
the underground lake,
have watched their studied dalliance
as they walked along its shore,
the gold-, silver-, diamond-spangled leaves
neither fluttering nor falling,
have heard their laughter
in the mirrored secret ballrooms,
can you be sure that the youngest is different?
Her sisters' eyes, you think,
are the colors of granite, and distant.

Star Gazer, now that you,
invisible, have come this far
to lose your heart,
gauge her laughter, her blush
as she reaches for the train of her silken gown,
looks past you with eyes
soft, you think, as the petals of flowers.
She moves gracefully into her partner's arms,
dances, her satin slippers flashing.
You, too, will be found out, you know.
You will have the kingdom and the choice.
She will want you then
and you will always disappoint.

DISTANT PLACES

The train that brought us here
will take us there

OWL

Outside
in the pine trees
this dark cold early morning
there is an owl
I hear him calling.

Now I feel
his silent flight,
the soft wings
like a giant moth's
lifting.

It is a different scale
of loneliness –
immense and patient.
Absolute.

Whoever I am
that is solitary
rises.

DRIVING HIGHWAY 15-501

How do I feel this morning?
Fine. I feel fine.
How do I feel this morning?
Sick with fear.
My teeth are separate stones.
My mouth tastes bitter.
Beside the highway
Each discarded tire grows fur,
Becomes a dead animal.
Each dead animal swings on my viscera
As on a plumbline.
The gas stations overtake me
Because I am afraid.

I am afraid of old phonograph records,
Photograph albums,
Maps,
Flowers pressed and drying in books,
Hymns.
I am afraid of the dead animals,
The highway.
Each morning.

BOULDER CREEK

The trail up Boulder Creek
Began on the canyon floor
In dust that settled on our boots
Like smoke,
In transparent snake skins,
The dry keening of cicadas,
And rose past chaparral
To a semblance of forest.

The creek was ordinary
Until we began to climb.
The thin waterfalls grew wider,
Roared into potholes,
Deep pools
The color of green glass.
High over the falls
The trail narrowed
To crumbling footholds,
On either side
Deer bones and the tracks
Of mountain lions.

There was a knife shining
At the bottom of the highest pool.
You stripped and dove for it,
Your body straight arrow white
Deep, deep through the green water.

I am writing this to tell you
The part of me that held back then
Now celebrates your act.
That thorny landscape
Seems a refuge.
The knife had seven blades.
Do you still have it?

FOR A HARD WINTER

This morning, light snow
dusted the cabin porch.
The mountains, soft-edged,
shapeless as old armchairs,
became less than clouds.
It has been weeks
Since you were here.
Who could draw comfort from that?
This is a fire
I can build alone.
I start with lighter wood
split crooked as the heart
around its little knots.

IN A PERUVIAN HAMMOCK

Across the courtyard wall
old women in fedoras and shawls
cup the sun to their faces
storing it for their bones.
The old men stand and spit
into the dusty road,
and brown, barechested children
chase chickens
under the few taxis that pass by.
It is an idle life,
and here we are as idle
as the green lizards
puffing and swaying
on the trunk of the shade tree,
more idle than that hairless dog
snapping at flies.

In the States
your father is a banker.
One of my grandfathers
was a stationmaster at eighteen –
he was that bright –
and his father a Quaker hatter.
Everyone measures money or time
or pious heads.
Not you and I.
When we are hungry
we have peaches and saltines
in the straw bag.
When we are sleepy, this hammock.
There is no need to hurry.
The train that brought us here
will take us there.

NIGHT PIECE

Clouds move across the sky
comfortable as smoke
from a neighbor’s woodstove.
The distant sounds of traffic
on the Interstate
are muffled in frost.
There are no streetlights
this far into the country.
The stars shine like steel.
They shift like iron filings.
They click an inhuman harmony.
Their mechanical destinies
are cold as clock parts.

HIKING LAUREL RIVER

1

Past the rapids,
in the pools,
white rocks,
the half-submerged backs
of old animals
waiting.

2

Water beetles,
metallic, dance
clicking in pairs –
erratic, erratic –
the way earrings
would like to do.

3

Mushrooms
insistent as babies' mouths.
Underneath
pale and puckered,
old lips
wanting kisses.

4

The hillside
in shadow.
Rhododendrons,
ferns, lichens
cascading,
green water
toward water.

ENDING

We are dead bees in a hive
that holds us.
We have made honey.
It lies in thick spoonfuls
at the bottom,
an amber deposit of the mornings
when we would gather, labor,
chew and spit.
It was an urgent manufacture,
and at night we guarded it,
sleeping back to back,
humming to each other.

GUEST HOUSE, RUHR UNIVERSITY

Would you have believed, father,
that human touch could heal?
This morning there is a mist
over the German landscape, and quiet.
During the night a warm wind,
up from the Mediterranean, settled
on the geraniums in the window boxes.
Now they are a softer red.
Under the duvet, I turn and am comforted;
comforted, am part of this world.

Out in the hall, Frau Stockmann
is not frantically dispensing bedlinen.
The Israelis above us are not shouting
across the telephone lines to grandmother.
The workmen who usually begin our days
with drills and hammers must be on holiday.
The Tanakas' baby sleeps.
We woke slowly to such peace.
I found that I had finally
dreamed you whole.

www.ingramcontent.com/pod-product-compliance
Ingram Content Group UK Ltd.
Pitfield, Milton Keynes, MK11 3LW, UK
UKHW041643190726
13854UKWH00006B/2662

9 798517 550804